MONDAY

TUESDAY

WEDNESDAY

THURSDAY

FRIDAY

AF256433

www.ingramcontent.com/pod-product-compliance
Lightning Source LLC
Chambersburg PA
CBHW080330030726
47593CB00010B/2958

* 9 7 8 1 0 8 8 1 9 0 9 7 5 *